D0648624

Until You Find
Strength

OTHER BOOKS BY
JASON F. WRIGHT

A MESSAGE OF COMFORT FOR WHEN
YOUR GRIEF FEELS TOO HEAVY

Until You Find *Strength*

JASON F. WRIGHT

SHADOW
MOUNTAIN
PUBLISHING

FOR YOU

© 2022 Jason F. Wright

All rights reserved. No part of this book may be reproduced in any form or by any means without permission in writing from the publisher, Shadow Mountain Publishing®, at permissions@shadowmountain.com. The views expressed herein are the responsibility of the author and do not necessarily represent the position of Shadow Mountain Publishing.

Visit us at shadowmountain.com

Library of Congress Cataloging-in-Publication Data

Names: Wright, Jason F., author.

Title: Until you find strength : a message of comfort for when your grief feels too heavy / Jason F. Wright.

Description: [Salt Lake City] : Shadow Mountain Publishing, [2022] | Summary: "An extended greeting-card to help those struggling with grief feel supported and comforted"—Provided by publisher.

Identifiers: LCCN 2021062764 | ISBN 9781629729954 (hardback)

Subjects: LCSH: Grief. | BISAC: SELF-HELP / Death, Grief, Bereavement | LCGFT: Self-help publications.

Classification: LCC BF575.G7 W754 2022 | DDC 152.4—dc23/eng/20220202

LC record available at https://lccn.loc.gov/2021062764

Printed in China

RR Donnelley, Dongguan, China

10 9 8 7 6 5 4 3 2 1

We love you Barnes family!
You are always the first to lift
to mourn with those that mourn and
to comfort those that stand in need of
comfort. We hope that we can do the
same for you whenever and however
you need it.
♡ The Hopkin Family
Alyssa, Eli, Eben, & Moira

♥

My friend, did you know you're on my mind today?

If you're holding this little book in your hands, I'm doing my best to hold your heart.

The people who love you, including me, know that you recently lost someone you loved.

No—not loved. *Love*. Now and forever.

And no matter who has left for a season,
the *quiet* will come.

Time will drip by in steady drops.

It looks like two a.m.

It feels like heavy, wet wool.

It sounds like familiar whispers and invisible footsteps in the kitchen.

We know how hard the quiet can be.

But we're still here.

After the services and the flowers
and the belated cards ...

When the freezer is finally empty of
those meals you didn't make...

When extended family and friends
return to their own homes ...

This season of grief can be the hardest.

But we're still here.

Routines resume. Life lumbers forward.

Your new normal has arrived. The one you didn't order.

But we're still here.

Yes, it's true. We're busy. Our lives are resuming too.

Our frantic race of responsibilities. The endless errands.

It feels like there's never enough time for
all the good our hearts hope to do.

Still, during this painful passage of time,
please know that we still *think of you often*.

We cheer for you!

We have faith in you!

Even if we don't call as
often as we should.

Or send that perfect message
at the perfect time.

Or knock on your door with
hot cookies and *warm hugs.*

We know your heart still aches.

And we're still here.

If too much time has passed,
please call.

We will come running.

If the quiet is unbearably loud, *send a text.*

Anytime, day or night, happy or sad emoji,
our *hearts* and phones await.

If you feel you might drown in your tears . . .

Or if surviving another day seems impossible,
reach out.

We will *embrace* you for
as long as you need.

Any hour. Any time. Any place.

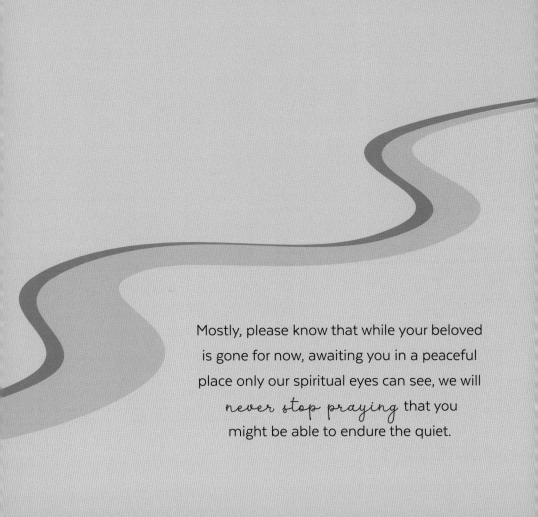

Mostly, please know that while your beloved
is gone for now, awaiting you in a peaceful
place only our spiritual eyes can see, we will
never stop praying that you
might be able to endure the quiet.

Because we *love you.*

We believe in you.

Because until you find strength,
we're still here.

And one day, somewhere down life's highway,
the sun will rise and bring *hope and healing*.

And we will still be here for you.

Feel loved.

Because you are.

AUTHOR'S NOTE

I've served as an ecclesiastical leader in various roles for years, and I have sat with many people in their grief. From noisy emergency rooms seconds after losing a loved one to quiet living rooms many months later, I've shared tears and advice with mourners.

Please note that I am not formally trained or licensed, and my counsel should not be considered professional advice, but I have seen several key principles work well.

Perhaps they might work for you too.

Do the Little Things

Keep the easy routines. Eat, sleep, walk. Watch your favorite shows. Even answer a few emails or texts if you can. Focusing on the little things you can control can help you during times when everything feels chaotic.

Those daily "you moments" can serve as a peaceful anchor in troubled waters.

Don't Fear the Laughter

When meeting with someone grieving, I often ask them to tell me a funny story about the loved one they've lost. It might be an embarrassing moment or the person's favorite—and often silly—joke.

The laughter almost always comes, and usually with a few tears.

Sometimes we worry that laughter can come too soon or too easily. It is okay to embrace the joy and memories that laughter brings. Laughter can be a happy tether to heaven.

Grieve As Needed

A friend once told me she felt like she was failing the mourning process. She'd seen others seem to heal quickly and get back on their feet with such ease.

Please know that our loved ones are not on the other side surrounded by angels holding grade books, judging us for how long it might take us to process our grief.

Our grief—like our life—is individual and personal. No passing is the same—each is a sacred and unique experience. So why would our grief need to look like anyone else's?

Embrace the Difficult Days

Eventually, with enough time, there will come a day when your grief is not so heavy nor so constant. You'll be back at work or school. You might have sold the home and moved away. You could even have fallen in love again.

While the most difficult days may be over, tough days will still come. Memories will resurface. Whether it's seeing your favorite photo, or recognizing a familiar smell, or even marking a date on the calendar, your grief will return. And when it does, don't push it away.

Embrace those difficult days and remind yourself just how much you loved that special person. So much so, that even after months, years, or decades, the loss is still there. You loved someone so deeply that, after all this time, you still miss them. *What a miracle.*

IMAGE CREDITS

P. 1   Vector Goddess/Shutterstock.com

P. 2   vladwel/Shutterstock.com

P. 4   Rostik Solonenko/Shutterstock.com

P. 6   GoodStudio/Shutterstock.com

P. 9   Darya Palchikova/Shutterstock.com

P. 10   GoodStudio/Shutterstock.com

P. 11   daisylove2507/Shutterstock.com

P. 13   Inkant/Shutterstock.com

P. 14   Dooder/Shutterstock.com,
        DiA99/Shutterstock.com

P. 15   Valentin Drull/Shutterstock.com

P. 16   MJgraphics/Shutterstock.com

P. 19   Ramcreative/Shutterstock.com

P. 20   Vector Goddess/Shutterstock.com